The Wisdom Trinity

Norman Habel

The Wisdom Trinity

An ancient Heresy worth Retrieving
or
An ancient Mystery worth Discerning

Norman Habel

Adelaide
2021

ISBN: 978-1-922582-28-7   soft
       978-1-922582-29-4   hard
       978-1-922582-30-0   epub
       978-1-922582-31-7   pdf

Published by:

An imprint of the ATF Press Publishing
Group owned by ATF (Australia) Ltd.
PO Box 234
Brompton, SA 5007
Australia
ABN 90 116 359 963
www.atfpress.com
Making a lasting impact

Table of Contents

Preamble
The Wisdom Trinity:
An ancient Heresy worth Retrieving

Three dimensions in one cosmic eco-system:

- **Primordial Wisdom**: the cosmic blueprint and sustaining impulse in creation
- **Innate Wisdom**: the driving force activating the realms and laws of nature
- **Incarnate Wisdom**: the spiritual compass guiding all living creatures

The Three 'Ways' of Wisdom:

An ancient Mystery worth Discerning

Three 'ways' (*derek*) collaborating in one cosmos

- **Primordial 'Way'**: the *derek* that enables a primordial power to design and sustain the cosmos
- **Nature 'Way'**: the innate *derek* that enables nature to function in tune with its laws
- **Incarnate 'Way'**: the innate *derek* that enables living creatures to act wisely and discern Wisdom

Introduction
My Wisdom Mentor

Discovering My Mentor

Over the years I have been fascinated by the Book of Job as a profound work of the Wisdom School of the ancient Near East. During that time, I used a range of hermeneutical tools and series of diverse lenses to read this amazing literary classic. In my eighties I have come to realise that there is another dimension of this book as a Wisdom text that I had not fully appreciated, a dimension I shall reveal as I explore the Wisdom Trinity.

In 1985 I produced a major commentary on the Book of Job that was published by Westminster Press. In that work, I employed literary criticism to highlight the brilliant literary design of the work. I wrote,

> Our concern is not primarily with identifying the remnants of ancient literary forms embedded in the text, but with the unique way in which forms, poetic patterns, structures and language are transformed and made subservient to the governing design or focus of a particular unit. 'Design' implies both the structured ordering of materials and an intention on the part of the author as a literary artist to create such and ordering (Habel, 1985, 23).

Some years later, when I was working with chaplains and other religious leaders, I developed an unpublished workbook entitled *Job, Jennifer and Jesus*. The aim of the workbook was for people who had suffered spiritual abuse to follow the journey of Job through the various stages of his traumatic experiences. In more recent times, I have explored how these traumatic experiences were handled by a figure designated the divine Wisdom therapist who interrogates Job from the whirlwind.

In 2014, after developing the principles of eco-hermeneutics I wrote an eco-wisdom reading of Job, entitled *Finding Wisdom in Nature*. The relevance of this research is apparent in the following statement:

> Because the Book of Job is a volume in the genre in the volume of works known as Wisdom Literature, I shall also focus on the diverse relationships between ecology and wisdom. Just as significant is my contention that the search for wisdom in creation, articulated in Job 28, is a determinative factor in the plot and perspective of the narrator of the Book of Job (Habel, 2014, 10).

My reference to the 'narrator of the Book of Job' is significant. Over the years I identified with the narrator as a literary artist, an empathetic colleague and a Wisdom theologian. I realise now that he is much more: he is my Wisdom Mentor and a radical critic.

Many are ready to identify with Job and his cruel sufferings at the hands of his God. Others may be fascinated by the way the trauma and healing of Job are portrayed. Many interpreters seek to explain the 'theology' of Job in the context of ancient Israel where the voices of the priests and prophets tended to override the voice of the wise.

However, many readers do not fully appreciate the role that the Wisdom narrator plays in the format and focus of the Book of Job. The narrator, I now believe, is not just describing the figure and fate of Job: the narrator is a mentor to Wisdom students and wise colleagues.

If I identify as one of those Wisdom students, I read more than a literary masterpiece or the portrait of traumatic suffering; I am invited to explore the world of Wisdom through the eyes of a Wisdom mentor. In the process I experience a Wisdom consciousness that enables me to 'discern' Wisdom in much the same way as Job.

My Wisdom mentor, if I am listening to one whom I perceive is an informed teacher, also confronts me with a range of beliefs and portrayals of YHWH, the God of Israel, that are inconsistent with a Wisdom worldview. From the perspective of the ancient covenant theology of Israel, the concept of a Wisdom trinity is tantamount to heresy. From the perspective of the Wisdom school, both the covenant theology of Moses and the ideology of the friends of Job are a hidden heresy.

Before I reveal the dimensions of the Wisdom trinity I perceive in the text, it is probably helpful to introduce the Wisdom school to which I believe my Wisdom mentor belongs.

My Mentor's Wisdom School

The Wisdom School refers to the thinking, techniques and traditions of a major body of citizens in ancient Israel known as 'the wise'. The wise were a discrete part of their community—distinct from the priests, prophets, royalty and other leading figures in their society. Whybray suggests that in Egypt and Israel there were actual 'schools' of wise men in locations like the royal court where they explored questions about how to pursue research, live wisely and give counsel to the leaders in society (1965, 16–17).

In the analysis pursued in this study, I will use the term 'Wisdom school' in its wider sense: referring to a Wisdom cosmology and *modus operandi* rather than to a specific school of royal scribes. The Wisdom school refers to an orientation that involves learning via critical observation and rational analysis, rather than revelation from a deity or a message from religious leaders. This school of thought included close observation of both the natural world and human behaviour. Wisdom thinking was akin to what today we would call 'scientific analysis': the wise were the 'scientists' of old, and they understood that the subject of their analysis was both a spiritual mystery and a natural reality.

Wisdom School Terminology

It is important to recognise, from the outset, that the Wisdom mentor incorporates specific technical terms that belong to the *modus operandi* and cosmology of the Wisdom school into the narrative. This terminology is tantamount to a message from my Wisdom mentor that the Book of Job has a specific Wisdom focus.

• **'design'** (*'etsa*)

'Design', when related to creation, may refer to the cosmic blueprint, the order, mystery and eco-system of the physical universe. According to Isaiah 46:10, YHWH's 'design' for the Earth is a primordial plan active from the very beginning of creation.

• **'observe'** (*ra'a*)

Like good scientists, the wise are expected to 'discern' through 'observation' and critical analysis. Their task is to 'observe' closely and discern the 'way': the determining innate characteristic of that phenomenon.

- **'discern'** *(bin)*

The verb 'discern' and the noun 'discernment' refer to the process of rational and critical analysis to ascertain the true essence of a subject, or to distinguish between the truth and falsity of a given reality. The aim of this act of discernment is to determine the 'way' (*derek*) and/or the 'place' *(maqom)* of a particular phenomenon of nature or society.

- **'acquire'** *(qana)*

To 'acquire' Wisdom is the mission and task of every student of Wisdom. Over the centuries, the wise observed the behaviour of humans, nature and society. Their observations led to an accumulation of acquired Wisdom known as proverbs. Observing and analysing nature— where Wisdom may be discerned as an innate force—is another way of acquiring Wisdom.

- **'place'** *(maqom)*

In the thinking of the Wisdom school, the ordering of phenomena on Earth ensures everything has its 'place'. The rocks of Earth, for example, are the 'place' of sapphires. It is central to the role of a student of the Wisdom school to determine the locus or 'place' of a given phenomenon in the world of nature. The ultimate question posed by the Wisdom school is 'Where can Wisdom be found? Where is its 'place' in the cosmos?

- **'way'** *(derek)*

Just as the term 'place' has Wisdom significance, so too does the key term *derek* (way) which is usually translated 'way'. Every living creature has its 'way' according to the school of Wisdom—a 'way' that is equivalent to a Wisdom compass embedded in a phenomenon of nature (Habel, 2015, 16).

Listening to My Mentor

In addition to inviting me to discern in the Wisdom terminology clues relating to the Wisdom focus and context, the Wisdom mentor uses diverse characters in speaking roles and, I believe, expects me to listen to the views they represent. These views range from the mischievous mindset of the Accuser in the heavenly council, to the wife of Job, to his three friends, and to Elihu, the brash young teenager.

The crucial clue for me, however, is the set of questions posed by the voice from the whirlwind. As a Wisdom student, those questions are directed at me via the person of Job. Every Wisdom student is expected to search for answers to these questions—answers that introduce the various dimensions of the Wisdom Trinity.

In the chapters that follow, I relate what I discern about the three dimensions of the Wisdom Trinity and then explore the implications of these findings in parallel 'heresies' within the Hebrew Scriptures.

A Clever Wisdom Critic

My Wisdom mentor is a clever critic living in the context of traditional teachings about YHWH, the God of Israel. These traditional teachings tend to suppress or counter the Wisdom tradition that my mentor is seeking to retrieve. It is well known that the scribes of Israel incorporated pre-Israelite traditions into the Hebrew Scriptures. In doing so, however, they often reworded the tradition by adding the name of YHWH and the thinking and understandings of the Israelite faith.

Many years ago, my research explored how Canaanite texts about the storm god Baal were adapted as hymns of praise for YHWH (Habel, 1964, 86–88). A famous example, Psalm 104, seems to be based on a fourteenth century Egyptian prototype, the *Great Hymn to Aton*. Psalm 29 is another good example:

> The voice of YHWH on the waters,
> the God of glory thunders.
> YHWH upon many waters,
> the voice of YHWH with power,
> the voice of YHWH with splendour (Ps 29:3–4).

Other significant examples are included in the Abraham legend: though this story cycle originates prior to the revelation of the name YHWH (Exod. 6:3–4), it is frequently retold with YHWH as a vital participant.

Segments of the pre-Israelite Abraham legends can be retrieved from Genesis 14 when Abraham celebrates a victory with the Canaanite priest Melchizedek, who pronounces a blessing:

> Blessed be Abram by El Elyon,
> maker of sky and land (Gen. 14:19).

It is apparent that Abraham recognises the Canaanite god El Elyon when he swears by that same god that he will not take advantage of his victory and will not take 'a thread or a sandal' that belongs to the king of Sodom (Gen. 14:20–24).

This Abraham legend is clearly pre-Israelite, even though later, when El makes a covenant with Abraham (Gen. 17:1–3), the Israelite editor modifies the name of the Canaanite god by adding the name YHWH (Habel, 2018, chapter 3).

I would argue, after listening to my Wisdom mentor's portrayal of Job and his world, the writer of this text is seeking to retrieve a pre-Israelite Wisdom tradition suppressed by YHWH believers. As part of this retrieval process—and in the context of Wisdom colleagues in the Wisdom school—the Wisdom narrator uses the jargon and journey of the characters in the Job narrative to expose the weaknesses of traditional beliefs.

At various points in my interaction with my Wisdom mentor, I will highlight the ways the Wisdom narrator undermines traditional Israelite teachings.

Procedure

My procedure in this study will be to explore the dynamic features of each of the three dimensions of Wisdom: Primordial Wisdom, Innate Wisdom, Incarnate Wisdom. I will also indicate briefly how a particular dimension of Wisdom outlined by the Wisdom narrator differs from traditional understandings of the same dimension elsewhere in the Hebrew Scriptures.

My starting point each of these chapters will the questions posed by the voice from the whirlwind (Job 38:1–3); as a student of the Wisdom school, I discern this is the voice of my Wisdom mentor.

My task is not merely to outline the distinctive features of the three dimensions of Wisdom. I discern that the Wisdom narrator, whom I have discovered is also my Wisdom mentor, is challenging me—and all Wisdom students—to use the questions posed from the whirlwind to both discern Wisdom in our contemporary world and to become Wisdom conscious.

Chapter One
Primordial Wisdom

Primordial Wisdom is the cosmic blueprint that
determines the design and creation of the cosmos.

Question One

The initial question I must face if I hear the voice of my
Wisdom mentor speaking through the voice echoing
from the whirlwind is:

Who is this who clouds my 'design' in darkness,
presenting arguments without knowledge (Job 38:2).

The focus of the first question relates to the primordial
'design' of the cosmos, and, by implication, is a question
that is relevant for the numerous questions that follow. I
am confronted with the need to be strong and explore the
mysteries of the primordial design of the cosmos.

The Testimony of Primordial Wisdom

To begin to appreciate the force of this question, I need
to turn to the declaration of Wisdom in her famous testimony in Proverbs 8, a testimony that preserves a pivotal
lesson of the Wisdom school.

The primordial remains a mystery that many cultures have long sought to understand, whether in terms of a specific divine presence or as an inherent primal impulse. In the Wisdom school, Wisdom represents a great mystery present in the primordial prior to creation. The question for me and contemporary Wisdom students is whether, following the lead of the Wisdom school, we will be able to discern that impulse alive in creation today as we adopt the *modus operandi* of the Wisdom school.

In the primordial we discover that, according to the Wisdom school, God 'acquires' Wisdom prior to the processes of creation. This is explicit in Proverbs 8 where Wisdom explains her nature and role in the primordial and thereafter. The following translation of Wisdom's opening words is a literal—and I believe accurate—rendering, unlike the interpretive versions found in many translations. Wisdom declares:

> YHWH acquired (*qana*) me first,
> his way (*derek*) before his works.
> From of old, from antiquity I was established,
> from the first, from the beginnings of Earth
> (Prov. 8:22–23).

Wisdom introduces herself as the 'way' that God 'acquires' before any of the works of creation. Wisdom is the primal 'way', the primal dimension or impulse in the pre-creation universe. The verb translated 'acquired' (*qana*) is the standard term employed in Proverbs for acquiring Wisdom (see Prov. 4:3, 7). The repeated injunction of the Wisdom teacher is to 'acquire Wisdom'! The aim of the wise is to 'acquire' Wisdom as an essential skill to discover, and follow the way of a positive life.

Given this context, it seems logical to understand this term in the standard way (compare Lenzi, 2006, 692). God 'acquires' Wisdom and in so doing is portrayed as a primordial sage, the ideal 'scientist,' the one who introduces the *modus operandi* of the wise as primal and powerful. God is introduced as the first student in, and founder of, the Wisdom school.

The primordial character of Wisdom is announced at several key points in her public testimony in Proverbs 8. She not only existed before the beginnings of Earth (Prov. 8:23), but she emerged or 'was brought forth' when there were no depths or mountains (Prov. 8:24–25). Wisdom was 'there' in the primordial before there were fertile fields or celestial realms (Prov. 8:26–28). Wisdom was 'beside' God even before the foundations of Earth were laid (Prov. 8:29–30). In short, Wisdom is introduced as a primordial impulse that existed before time, space or matter came into being, an impulse that is portrayed as the 'way' acquired by God in this Wisdom school text.

The 'Way' of Primordial Wisdom

Crucial for an appreciation of the nature and role of Wisdom in Proverbs 8—and elsewhere in Wisdom texts—is the designation of Wisdom as the 'way', the primordial formative force or factor that precedes the works of creation. In Proverbs 8, this *derek* is explicitly identified as Wisdom acquired by the creator.

The 'way' (*derek*) of something refers to its *bildende Kraft*, its own inner formative force—or, as I suggest, its driving characteristic (Habel, 2003, 286). Its *derek* is something's essential nature.

Scholars have long sought to discern precisely what this primal dimension might be. McKane declares:

> I would hold with von Rad that the intention here is to emphasize the vast intelligence of Wisdom by assigning to her an architectonic function in the ordering of the world (1970, 351).

I would argue, that if Wisdom is indeed the *derek* that this God 'acquires', it is the *derek* within God—and not God—that creates the cosmos. Wisdom, the 'way', precedes and enables the 'works' of creation. Primordial Wisdom is indeed the first dimension of Wisdom: the creative blueprint and cosmic impulse that precedes and activates creation. Wisdom is not a deity; Wisdom is the cosmic principle that precedes and enables creation.

As an aside, it is worth making a comparison with the Tao, of Taoism. The term 'tao' is regularly rendered 'way'. According to Wikipedia,

> Tao is the natural order of the universe, whose character one's human intuition must discern to realise the potential for individual wisdom.

A Wisdom version of this definition would read,

> *derek* (way) is the natural order (primordial Wisdom) of the cosmos, whose presence and character one's incarnate human Wisdom must 'discern' to realise the potential for individual Wisdom.

Question Two

When we return to the questions the Wisdom mentor is posing through the voice from the whirlwind, the answers at first seem obvious. But, are they?

> Where were you when I laid Earth's foundation?
> Tell if you have gained 'discernment!
> Who fixed its dimensions? Surely you know!
> Or who stretched out the measuring line over it?
> On what were its pillars sunk?
> Or who set its cornerstone
> when the morning stars sang together
> and all the sons of God shouted for joy? (Job 38:4–7).

The opening line seems to suggest that the Creator was the one who laid Earth's foundations, even though each of the following verses pose the question: Who?

Crucial for understanding this question is the reference to 'discernment'. Job and I are expected to exercise our Wisdom compass to 'discern' the answer: the Wisdom factor in the construction of Earth is an integral component in the 'design' of the cosmos.

The design of the cosmos, not the deity, is pivotal.

Question Three

The mentor also asks us to explore frightening realms in the depths of the cosmos— realms that are not only beyond the control of humans, but also represent the terrifying world of the Deep.

> Have you penetrated the sources of Sea,
> or walked through the recesses of the Deep?
> Have the gates of Death been revealed to you?
> Have you seen the gates of Death's gloom?
> Have you 'discerned' the expanses of Earth?
> Tell me if you know all this? (Job 38:16–18).

Just as scientists today seek to penetrate the extremities of the cosmos, the limits of outer space, and the depths of dark matter, we are challenged by our Wisdom mentor to locate the extremities of space, light and darkness. We are confronted with facing a journey into what, in the days of the Wisdom school, was the underworld that included the domains of Death

Especially significant is the question about 'discerning' the 'expanses' of Earth. Ancient Wisdom school scientists discern dimensions of Wisdom by close investigation and observation, not by faith or tradition. Now, in the twenty-first century, we Wisdom seekers are challenged, with Job, to employ our Wisdom skills to grasp the extremities of Earth in the design of the cosmos—and in realms beyond where humans can normally 'observe' nature.

The 'Orthodox' Tradition

From the perspective of the traditional Israelite understanding of the process of creation, the portrayal of Primordial Wisdom in the book of Job may well be considered a heresy. According to the classic declaration of Psalm 33,

> By the Word of YHWH the heavens were made,
> and all the host by the breath of his mouth.
> Let all the Earth fear the Lord,
> let all the inhabitants of the world stand in awe of him!
> For he spoke and it came to be;
> he commanded and it stood forth (Ps 33:6–8).

According to this tradition, it is YHWH, the God of Israel, who created heaven and Earth by almighty word, not by 'acquiring Wisdom'. The entire world is expected to stand in awe of YHWH because YHWH's powerful creative voice—not the acquisition and implementation of Primordial Wisdom—created everything.

The narrative version of creation in Genesis 1 reflects an editing of the text that presents the Creator's word creating segments of the cosmos. The Creator says, 'Let there be light', 'Let there be a firmament', and so on. An ancient tradition about creation has, it seems, been made consistent with creation by the Word of the Creator by the addition of a series of pronouncements: 'And God said . . .

Significantly, however, the Creator does not say 'Let there be 'Earth/Land': Land, like Wisdom, is pre-existent in the Deep, and emerges from the primordial waters like a baby being born (Gen. 1:9–11). Once she is born, the Creator names the baby 'Land'.

Afterthought

I have long heard
'the cosmos was created by the Word of YHWH'
but now I discover
'Wisdom was a creative impulse long before
any modes of creation'.

Chapter Two
Innate Wisdom

Innate Wisdom is the driving force that governs the realms and laws of nature.

Question One

Whenever I listen to the voice of my Wisdom mentor in the famous interrogation of Job from the whirlwind, I am confronted with questions of discernment that have long challenged me.

Perhaps the most frequent question, often with a measure of humour, is:

Who put Wisdom in the clouds?
Who gave Discernment to my pavilion? (Job 38:36).

Traditionally, the 'orthodox' reader would simply respond by saying 'God'; 'God is the Creator Spirit who put Wisdom in the clouds and all the realms of nature.'

In the wider Wisdom context of these questions from my Wisdom mentor and the famous *Wisdom Magna Carta* of Job 28, however, it becomes apparent that Wisdom is innate in the forces of nature.

The *Wisdom Magna Carta*

The Wisdom narrator of the book of Job did not only find an imaginative way to relate the dialogue between Job and his friends; the narrator inserted a crucial chapter that has been designated the *Wisdom Magna Carta*. The focus of this independent chapter linked to the primordial is innate Wisdom: Wisdom is a driving force in the realms of nature.

The *Wisdom Magna Carta* is a vivid portrait of where and how a model ancient Wisdom scientist—a clever creation of the Wisdom narrator—discerned Wisdom innate in the driving forces and realms of nature.

The 'Place' of Wisdom

The ultimate question posed in this *Wisdom Magna Carta* is: Where can Wisdom be found? Or, in other words, what is the 'place' of Wisdom in the ecosystem of the cosmos? Crucial for an understanding of this tradition is the Wisdom school concept of 'place' (*maqom*), the locus or habitat of a phenomenon in the ecosystem network of the universe. In the design of creation there is an appointed 'place' for each realm, creature or component of nature.

In the *Wisdom Magna Carta*, the Wisdom school narrator, tackles the question of the essential 'place' of everything in the universe and asks the question: Where is the 'place' of Wisdom herself? The answer to that question might seem obvious: the source or the original 'place' of Wisdom is within God.

In the course of this poem, however, the Wisdom narrator leads us on a search that ends in another location—the world of nature!

The opening verse of this *Wisdom Magna Carta* immediately focuses on the question of the 'place' of various phenomena in creation: entities such as silver and gold:

> Truly, there is a source for silver
> and a 'place' for the gold they refine (Job 28:1).

As indicated above, everything has its appointed 'place' in the order of creation, and more specifically on Earth. Gold has its 'place' in Earth (Job 28.1); precious gems have their 'place' in stones (v.6); rocks too have a 'place' on Earth (Job 14.18); Earth has its 'place' in the cosmos (Job 9.6); and each mortal has a 'place' on Earth (Job 7.10).

By establishing that precious commodities have a specific 'place' in the design of the universe, the Wisdom narrator prepares the way for posing the ultimate question about the 'place' of Wisdom, the most precious find of all (Job 28.12).

The Wisdom sought in this *Magna Carta* is of far greater value than any other precious commodity. A knowledge of Wisdom innate in nature can only be acquired by the skills of close observation and critical analysis as demonstrated by the Wisdom Scientist of the *Wisdom Magna Carta*.

Discerning the 'Way' of Wisdom

In the final verses of the *Wisdom Magna Carta*, the Wisdom narrator imagines God to be the one who first undertook a successful search for Wisdom. This imagined divine Sage-cum-Scientist is depicted as searching far and wide across Earth to find Wisdom. Unlike other deities of the ancient world who claimed to possess great Wisdom, the god portrayed by the narrator of the Wisdom school searches for Wisdom.

In the ancient Near East, the god Ea was known as 'the wisest of the gods who knew every sort of thing'. The wisdom of Marduk was considered a mystery never understood by humans. And the sun god, Shamash, was not only wise and mighty; 'he was his own counsellor' (Kalugila, 1980, 30–45).

The 'place' where the divine Sage of the *Wisdom Magna Carta* begins to search for Wisdom is surprising: it is not a distant realm among the gods or the council of heaven. The 'way' of Wisdom that the Wisdom 'scientist,' discerns is not in the 'mind' of God or a personal divine capacity. Rather,

> God 'discerned' (*bin*) her 'way' (*derek*),
> and came to know her 'place' (*maqom*),
> for God looked to the ends of Earth
> and 'observed' (*ra'a*) everything under heaven (Job 28:23–24).

The model divine scientist is here portrayed as searching the ends of Earth, including every realm 'under heaven'. The model Wisdom scientist 'observes', 'discerns' and thereby scrutinises the entire landscape of the planet. The 'place' of Wisdom is on/in Earth!

Findings of Innate Wisdom Research

When we finally reach the climax of the *Wisdom Magna Carta*, God, the imagined Wisdom scientist, is portrayed by the Wisdom narrator as discovering Wisdom in nature.

This discovery of Wisdom, however, is not depicted as a recent event. It is specifically linked to the origin of the meteorological realms in the cosmos. These specific domains, it would seem, are representative of all the realms of nature.

> When God fixed the **weight** of the wind
> and meted out the waters by **measure**,
> when God made a **law** (*choq*) for the rain
> and a **way** (*derek*) for the thunderstorm,
> then God observed (*ra'a*) her and appraised her,
> established her and probed her (Job 28:25–27).

A crucial focus of the search for Wisdom portrayed in the *Wisdom Magna Carta* is not the specific realms of nature themselves. It is an innate feature of these realms where Wisdom is to be found and with which Wisdom is identified. The use of the technical terms 'way' (*derek*) and 'rule/law' (*choq*) identify the innate character of these phenomena—whether it be in the wind, the waters, the storms or the rain.

The Wisdom Scientist Model

The model Wisdom scientist does not merely 'observe' a given phenomenon. The scientist 'discerns' its 'way' (*derek*), its inner code, its innate character. By discerning the 'ways' of these phenomena of nature, the Wisdom scientist discovers innate Wisdom.

Wisdom, then, is not separate from these phenomena of nature. Wisdom is a driving force, an innate dimension of nature. By employing the research methods identified in the *Wisdom Magna Carta*, a student or scientist of the Wisdom school can discover Wisdom as a 'network of forces in nature'.

Question Two

My Wisdom mentor summons me to answer additional questions about the presence and role of innate Wisdom in the realms of nature. In line with the findings of the *Wisdom Magna Carta*, my Wisdom mentor asks,

> Do you know the 'way' of lightning flashes
> and how the East wind blows across the Earth?
> Who cleft a channel for the torrents
> and the 'way' for the thunderstorm? (Job 38:24–25).

In Job 28:22–30 the Wisdom mentor poses a range of questions about the weather, every realm: from storehouses for snow, to flashes of lightning, from floods in wastelands to heavy rains, from the hoarfrost in the sky to ice freezing over the Deep. These questions are essentially answered by the findings in the *Wisdom Magna Carta,* outlined above. All the meteorological realms of nature have innate Wisdom, the '*derek*' that governs their function.

Question Three

Perhaps the most challenging question relates to the laws of nature and the constellations found in space—a question that modern astrophysicists may find challenging, too.

> Can you bind the fetters of Pleiades
> or loosen the reins of Orion?
> Can you lead out Mazzaroth in its season
> or guide the Bear with her sons?
> Do you know the 'laws' of the skies?
> Can you establish their order on Earth?
> (Job 38:31–33).

The initial challenge is to probe traditional knowledge of the constellations. It is one thing to observe and wonder at their design and pattern in the sky; it is quite another to contemplate how these constellations in space are controlled by a dimension of Wisdom that is beyond human ingenuity. The Wisdom narrator views the skies as a realm filled with both mystery and mythology, and the scientific and the spiritual.

Even more stunning, perhaps, is the question posed about the 'laws' (*chuqoth*) of the skies (Job 38:33). The focus is clearly on Wisdom as science, not on some deity who controls the heavens or manipulates the stars.

We might identify the laws in the skies governing the cosmos with contemporary understandings of gravity and astral forces. Just as Wisdom is found by the divine

Wisdom scientist in the 'laws' of nature associated with the weather (Job 28:25–26), Job, I—and all Wisdom students—are now challenged to discern the same Wisdom functioning in the laws of space.

The Wisdom narrator asks whether the laws of space can be employed to establish ordered realms on Earth— a genuine mystery apparent in both ancient ecology and astrophysics.

This question relates to the very core of ecology as a science: How do the laws of one realm interrelate with those of another realm? How do the laws of space interact and affect the *modus operandi* of planet Earth? How do the laws of the cosmos relate to each other to facilitate the operation of the universe and the place of Earth in that universe? How does the cosmos function?

In short, we is confronted with one of the great mysteries of astrophysics: the cosmic ecology of time, space and matter!

Alternative Traditions

The clear and bold portrayal of Wisdom as the innate 'way' (*derek*) in all the realms and laws of nature, stands in stark contrast to the so-called 'orthodox' traditions. That the Wisdom narrator regards these traditions as problematic is apparent in the way they are presented via the voices of the characters in the book of Job. These voices precede our invitation to discern the innate character of Wisdom in the Wisdom mentor's radical questions to Job.

The Celestial Overlord

The first voice we hear is that of a god who functions as a celestial overlord who manipulates nature to compliment this god's ego. In a satirical scene set in the council of heaven, the overlord allows a celestial opponent to employ the forces of nature to overwhelm an innocent human on Earth. The human involved is Job whose entire family is destroyed by fire, leaving Job with a body full of boils and a wife who proposes he 'curse God and die' (Job 1–2).

Job is identified as one of the wise, but the god portrayed by the Wisdom narrator is willing to permit unjustified disasters in order to win a bet with the celestial opponent who monitors the course of events on Earth.

The opening scene, therefore, is how the Wisdom narrator sets the stage for unravelling the 'ways' of Wisdom. The narrator exposes this celestial overlord as a selfish deity who does not employ or discern Wisdom in decision-making.

The Righteous Ruler

Perhaps the most dominant deity found in the speeches of Job's three friends is the righteous ruler. The Wisdom narrator portrays this deity as a god of reward and retribution in accord with the Sinai covenant. This deity is depicted as readily using the realms of nature to reward the faithful with blessings and strike the wicked with divine retribution.

In the words of Eliphaz, the god El is a deity who dispenses blessings on the faithful

> If it were me, I would seek El
> and commit my case to God
> who does great inscrutable deeds
> wonders beyond reckoning,
> who gives rain upon the Earth
> and sends waters across the countryside (Job 5:8–10).

El is here and elsewhere in the Hebrew Scriptures depicted as the generous ruler who dispenses blessings such as rain across the landscape. Earth is dependent on the blessings of the god El for fertility and beauty.

According to Zophar, this god possesses all the secrets of Wisdom and if he dared to expound them, Job would learn that 'God extracts from you less than your guilt demands' (Job 11:6). Eliphaz describes in great detail how the punishment of El terrifies the wicked, overwhelming them with darkness and despair (Job 15:17–35). Bildad predicts that El will destroy the wicked with fire and brimstone (Job 18:5–21). El, the god of reward and retribution, displays power radically different from that of Wisdom; Wisdom's power is innate in the realms of nature.

Initially Job, too, is depicted as being deluded by this traditional god of the friends. Job recognises not only that this god possesses Wisdom but that this deity's almighty power overwhelms this god's Wisdom and creates havoc on Earth. The Wisdom narrator demonstrates that this deity misuses the waters as forces of destruction. The Wisdom school's truth is that 'Wisdom' is the *derek* in the waters that governs their functions in nature.

> With him are Wisdom and power,
> his are counsel and understanding.
> When he breaks down there is no rebuilding;
> when he imprisons there is no release.
> When he holds back the waters they dry up;
> when he lets them loose, they overthrow the Earth
> (Job 12:13–15).

The Watcher of Humans

Job's experience of the god he has known, according to the Wisdom narrator, is not as a god who only punishes the wicked, but also as a god who delights in viewing the fate of innocent victims like Job. He accuses this god of being a 'Watcher of Humans'—a divine 'seeing Eye' (Job 7:8). Job declares,

What are mortals that you exalt them
and set your heart on them?
You visit them every morning
and test them every instant.
How long before you lift your face from my gaze
and allow me swallow my spittle?
Assume I sin! How do I harm you,
O Watcher of Humans? (7:17–20).

This passage is not only a vivid portrait of the god that Job experiences as a distant observer, a Watcher of Humans. It is also parody of the hymnic version of the *imago Dei* in Psalm 8.

What is man that you should remember him,
mortal man that you should visit (*pqd*) him?
You made him a little less than a god,
crowning him with honour and glory (Ps 8:5–6 NEB).

For Job, the *imago Dei* tradition is a false dream. The god who 'visits' Job belittles rather than exalts, humiliates rather than glorifies, induces trauma rather than potential (Habel, 1985, 165).

By allowing Job to belittle the *imago Dei*, the Wisdom narrator shows Job is undermining traditional teachings expounded by his friends.

In contrast to the friends' traditional Israelite portrayals of their god in their dialogues, Job's god is the Wisdom scientist discovers Wisdom innate in nature. Job's god-as-Wisdom scientist may seem heretical to a traditional worshipper of YHWH.

Afterthought

I have long heard
'the sound of thunder is a sign of YHWH's coming judgement',
but now I discover
'the sound of thunder is the pulse of innate Wisdom'.

Chapter Three
Incarnate Wisdom

Incarnate Wisdom is the Innate Spiritual compass enabling all living creatures to act wisely and discern Wisdom.

Question One

The final question reported by our Wisdom mentor relates to that dimension of Wisdom that we have here identified at 'Incarnate Wisdom'. We are confronted with the dimension of Wisdom that is innate in living creatures such as hawks and eagles.

> Is it by your 'discernment' that the hawk soars,
> spreading his wings to the South?
> Does the eagle mount at your command
> and build his nest on high?
> He makes his dwelling on a rock,
> on a rocky crag his stronghold.
> From there he searches for food,
> from afar his eyes detect it (Job 39:26–29).

The Wisdom mentor progressively moves the focus of the questions: from the primordial and inanimate realms of the cosmos to the world of living creatures; from Primordial and Innate Wisdom, to what I have identified as Incarnate Wisdom—the guiding compass in living beings, especially those in the wild. Both the hawk and the eagle have Incarnate Wisdom: the innate discernment that enables them to spread their wings and soar, to construct a stronghold on a rocky crag, and detect food below from their world on high.

Wisdom as the Incarnate 'Way'

The background to the first question posed by the Wisdom narrator is the concept of Wisdom as the incarnate *'derek'* in living creatures. A clear illustration of this Wisdom school concept is evident when the wise mentor encourages that novice to observe the distinctive code behaviour of the ant:

> Go to the ant, you lazybones!
> 'Observe' its 'way' and be wise!
> Without having any chief
> or officer or ruler,
> it prepares its food in summer,
> and gathers its sustenance in harvest (Prov. 6:6–8).

The Wisdom Incarnate (the 'way') in an ant colony is, according to these ancient scientists, an inner capacity to function as a corporate body without any hierarchy— without any bosses or leaders: a mystery that modern scientists still find fascinating.

Another dimension of incarnate ant Wisdom, according to this ancient scientist, is its instinctual/intellectual capacity to gather food wisely in summer and store it for the winter when conditions for finding food are difficult. The Wisdom embedded in the ant is a compass that enables it to anticipate the future and plan ahead (Habel, 2013, 3).

It may seem surprising that ants were chosen by the wise as an exemplar of Wisdom Incarnate in living creatures on our planet. I was delighted to discover that Tim Flannery, in his chapter on 'super-organisms', also explores the amazing innate capacity of ants, especially attine ants, to construct complex ecosystems we might call societies: agricultural societies. Consistent with the biblical quotation above, Flannery describes the corporate intelligence of ants as follows:

> While pheromones allow ant colonies to behave in 'intelligent' ways, theirs is an intelligence of a very particular kind. No ant carries around a blueprint of the social order in its head, unlike we do, and there is no overseer or 'brain caste' that regulates the colony's activities. Instead, ants create strength from weakness by pooling their individually limited capacities into a collective decision-making system that bears an uncanny resemblance to our own democratic process (2010, 115).

The wise of the Wisdom school would correct Flannery's research, however, and maintain they do not create strength out of weakness: ants possess a strong incarnate force known as Wisdom that enables them to design a coherent ant colony.

The wise in ancient Wisdom Schools called this interconnected and programmed intelligence of ants the 'way' or Wisdom dimension of the ant. And as Flannery outlines, this inner capacity is apparent in all areas of the ant ecosystem—from the ingenious techniques used to locate and prepare a new habitat to the sophisticated practices developed for the agriculture of fungus. These inner capacities may have developed over millions of years, but they testify to a deep dimension of such creatures in nature that may surely be designated their Incarnate Wisdom (Habel, 2013, 3–4).

Though there is a range of Wisdom texts that focus on 'hearing' the Wisdom of the mentor or of a relevant tradition, central to the 'scientific' orientation of the Wisdom school, however, is the practice of 'seeing/observing' Wisdom innate in nature. Fundamental to the mystery of Wisdom in nature is that every phenomenon and domain of nature has an innate code (*derek*) or law that governs its characteristic behaviour as an integral part of an ecosystem. The 'way' of things is the innate code of Wisdom intelligence that governs their behaviour.

The author of Proverbs 30 explores a range of Wisdom mysteries both in society and in nature. The author claims to lack the capacity to understand the mysteries, the innate 'ways' that are apparent (Prov. 30:1–3). The author declares there are four 'ways' in nature that are too wonderful to comprehend:

> The way of an eagle in the sky,
> the way of a snake on a rock,
> the way of a ship on the high seas,
> the way of a man with a girl (Prov. 30:18–19).

Question Two

When Job is led by the Wisdom narrator into the kingdom of the wild he is confronted by the ways of the living creatures of the wild. The assumption is that these creatures have an Incarnate Wisdom that enables them to survive in the wild; my Wisdom mentor asks,

> Do you know the time when the ibex give birth?
> Do you watch over the calving of hinds?
> Can you count the months they must fulfil?
> Do you know the time of their delivery,
> when they crouch to deliver their young
> and drop their offspring?
> Their young are healthy; they grow up in the open;
> they leave and never return (Job 39:1–4).

The wild ibex are portrayed not only as having the necessary Wisdom to deliver their young at the right time, but also as having the young who possess the necessary Wisdom to leave their parents and become healthy adults on their own. Ironically, the ostrich does not seem to possess the same degree of Wisdom to care for her young (Job 39:13–17).

Question Three

At certain pivotal points the Wisdom narrator poses questions that are more than another example of Innate or Incarnate Wisdom. The questions challenge an orthodox tradition of the wider Israelite community. With delicious irony, the narrator has God asking Job whether he could get the wild ox to be his baby-sitter or serve as his servant in the field:

> Is the wild ox willing to serve you?
> Will he spend the night beside your crib?
> Can you hold the wild in furrows with ropes?
> Will he harrow the valleys behind you?
> Can you trust him to harvest you grain
> and gather it from the threshing floor? (Job 39:9–12).

The significance of this challenge is not only the emphasis on the independence and identity of the ox as a creature whose 'place' is in the wild, but also on the challenge to a major biblical tradition: the 'mandate to dominate' found in Genesis 1:26–28 (Habel, 2009, chapter 1). In this Genesis passage, humans are created in the image of God, which gives them the right to 'suppress Earth' and 'have dominion over' all animal creatures (compare Habel, 2001). This anthropocentric text is inconsistent with the natural ecosystem of planet Earth. The challenge of Job 39:9 explicitly undermines the theological mandate of

Genesis 1:26–28 and recognises an ecology of human–
animal relationships that is discerned by the Wisdom
school through their observation of Wisdom in nature.
The Incarnate Wisdom in the wild ox means that they will
not 'serve' humans who, from a traditional Israelite perspective, are to 'rule' over all creatures.

Traditions under Attack

Throughout the text of the book of Job, the Wisdom
narrator has voices debating teachings that are in conflict with the Wisdom Trinity worldview being explored
through Job's journey.

In his first speech, Eliphaz claims to have a religious
experience that justifies his teaching:

> Can mortals be righteous before God,
> Humans pure before their maker?
> If he does not trust his own servants,
> and ascribes no glory to his angels,
> what then of those who dwell in clay houses,
> whose foundation are in the dust,
> who are crushed before a moth (Job 4:17–19).

Rather than possessing Innate Wisdom, humans are
described as created by God with incarnate sin: they have
an innate impulse to be unrighteous rather than wise.
This teaching has been identified as 'original sin'; voiced
by one of the discredited friends, the narrator is identi-
fying this as a false doctrine to students of the Wisdom
school.

Given the disasters and trauma he experiences, Job is
portrayed by the narrator as struggling to reach his Incarnate Wisdom, which he designates as his *derek*, his 'way'.

> Why is life given to a person whose 'way' is hid,
> hedged around by Eloah? (Job 3:23).

While Job recognises that he indeed has an incarnate *derek*, his suffering is such that his Incarnate Wisdom seems to be hidden by his God. In outlining the course of Job's journey, the Wisdom narrator explores how Job becomes free to express his Incarnate Wisdom.

In spite of their connection with Job as one of the wise, Job's friends, notably Eliphaz, still echo the traditional understanding of the beginning of Wisdom. They accuse Job of abusing the fear of God with his allegations of divine brutality.

> Should a wise man answer with wind for knowledge
> and fill the belly with an East Wind?
> Yet you, you subvert the fear of God,
> you diminish devotion towards El.
> Were you the first human ever born?
> Were you brought forth even before the hills?
> Did you listen in on the council of God
> and keep Wisdom for yourself? (Job 15:2–8).

Eliphaz is accusing Job of an arrogant claim to possess Wisdom as a secret word overheard in the primordial council of God. Eliphaz is charging Job with the claim that 'he is the beginning', the first to possess Wisdom— and, in so doing, 'subverting the fear of God'.

In a strange twist, towards the end of the book of Job, Elihu, the impudent teenager, challenges all his elders about their knowledge of Wisdom. He declares Wisdom is the spirit incarnate in humans: Wisdom does not come with age but is the 'breath of Shaddai' deep within a human being that activates insight/Wisdom.

> I am young in days and you are old men,
> so I was scared and afraid to speak my mind before
> you.
> I said to myself, 'Days will testify
> and many years teach Wisdom!'

Surely she is the spirit in humans
and the breath of Shaddai gives them insight
(Job 32:6–8).

The Orthodox Tradition

Many Wisdom school traditions have been revised in line with the Israelite faith in YHWH, the covenant God of Israel; they do not focus on Incarnate Wisdom, but on a prior subordinate relationship with YHWH. As the classic injunction reads,

> The fear of YHWH is the beginning of Wisdom
> and knowledge of the Holy One is insight (Prov. 9:10).

In this tradition, Wisdom is not incarnate in humans or other living creatures; Wisdom is dependent on 'fear of YHWH'.

As early as 1972, I demonstrated that the first nine chapters of Proverbs are a re-interpretation of the original Wisdom school tradition to make them consistent with traditional Israelite religion. A clear illustration of this re-interpretation is found in the opening verses of Proverbs 2. After the common protasis of Proverbs 2:1–4, we can distinguish two apodoses that illustrate how the original tradition was made orthodox by a traditional Israelite re-reading that focused on YHWH.

Apodosis A: Prov. 2:9–11	Apodosis B: Prov. 2:5–8
Then (*'oz*) **You will understand** what is right and just and straight; every good track.	Then (*'oz*) **You will understand** the fear of YHWH and find the knowledge of God.

For (*ki*)	For (*ki*)
Wisdom will enter your heart and **knowledge** will delight your inner self.	YHWH gives **Wisdom** and **knowledge** and understanding come from his mouth.
Ingenuity will **protect** you, understanding will **guard** you.	So as to **guard** the paths of justice, and **protect** the way of the faithful.

According to the 'orthodox' YHWH tradition, Wisdom is not an innate or incarnate dimension of a human being or any other living being. On the contrary, the fear of YHWH originates from the Wisdom that YHWH imparts.

The original Wisdom school tradition does not link Incarnate Wisdom with YHWH. Wisdom and knowledge enter the heart and become part of human nature quite independently. From there they both guide the person's understanding of what is right and what protects a person from within. In the original Wisdom school tradition, Wisdom is incarnate, not imposed by YHWH.

Conclusion

The Wisdom mentor makes it quite clear that the 'Fear of YHWH' is not the beginning of Wisdom.

Far more profound is an understanding of the truth, in Wisdom terms: Wisdom is incarnate in all living creatures—everything from an ox to an eagle, from an ibex to an ant, from a lion to a human.

Wisdom has its beginning deep within each living being from the moment of birth.

That is the mystery Job and I have to learn and now explore.

Afterthought
I have long heard
'the fear of YHWH is the beginning of Wisdom'
but now I discover
'the beginning of Wisdom precedes the fear of YHWH'.

Chapter Four
Wisdom Consciousness

Wisdom consciousness involves an acute discernment of the presence, power and significance of Wisdom in all the realms of our environment.

The Omnipresence of Wisdom

The questions posed by the Wisdom narrator, who functions as my Wisdom mentor, ranged from the primordial, to realms of the cosmos, to the environment, to the laws of nature, to living creatures of the wild and to the innate *derek* of human beings like Job. Wisdom is indeed omnipresent—present as the primordial blueprint; as the governing force in the realms of nature; as the compass guiding living beings to be true to their nature.

The dilemma we face as orthodox believers is to assume the omnipresence of our God as our point of departure. The omnipresent God has the capacity to be located anywhere and everywhere in the diverse realms of the universe.

Wisdom, however, as we have discovered through the Wisdom narrator, is 'in' all the realms of the cosmos, permeating, activating and animating these realms as parts of a cosmic ecosystem.

Rather than focusing on the mystery of God's invisible omnipresence, the Wisdom narrator is challenging us to discern Wisdom as a captivating mystery that is in, with and under all that we see, hear, touch and wonder about.

Activating Wisdom Consciousness

Given the mystery of Wisdom omnipresent in our contemporary world, how do we activate our Wisdom consciousness to discern Wisdom in the wonders and mysteries of the world around us?

If we return to the opening challenge of the voice from the whirlwind we might simply follow the lead of many interpreters and identify this as a theophany (Job 38:1–3).

If, however, we recognise what the Wisdom narrator has done to attract Job's attention, we realise that focus in not on a manifestation of the presence of God: a theophany. The focus is on questions designed to awaken Job's consciousness so that he can discern Wisdom and answer questions about the 'design' of the cosmos.

The questions from the whirlwind are more than a cosmic quiz designed to test Job's knowledge; they are a provocation, a means of activating Job's discernment, his capacity to discern answers that relate to Wisdom, the primordial design of the cosmos.

When Job finally responds to the challenging questions relating to the presence and function of Wisdom in creation, he confesses,

> You said,
> 'Who is this who obscures my 'design' without knowledge?'
> Indeed, I spoke without 'discernment,'
> of things beyond, which I did now know (Job 42:3)

Job admits that, prior to his cosmic journey exploring the dimensions and realms of Wisdom, he had not employed his inner capacity—his Incarnate Wisdom—to discern the mystery of Wisdom functioning throughout his world. And my Wisdom mentor is challenging me, as Job's Wisdom companion, to admit that I too have been dependent on prior knowledge rather than the immediate discernment of the mystery of Wisdom functioning in my world.

In Chapter One, my Wisdom mentor took me back to the beginnings of creation to join Job in discerning Wisdom as the primordial blueprint in the design and creation of the cosmos.

How might I, today, in the twenty-first century, discern the presence of Primordial Wisdom in my world?

If I dare to explore the galaxies of the universe and reach back in time to the primordial, I may also become aware that the cosmos of which I am a minute fragment, has been guided by the force of Wisdom from before the Big Bang. I may gain a cosmic consciousness that is tantamount to a cosmic Wisdom consciousness. I, too, may be motivated—by the questions from the whirlwind—to discern Wisdom in my cosmos.

In Chapter Two, my Wisdom mentor revealed how Wisdom is innate in all realms and laws of nature. The *Wisdom Magna Carta*, deliberately inserted by the Wisdom narrator into the book of Job, provided a model of how, if my discernment is aroused to become Wisdom conscious like the divine Wisdom scientist, I can discern Wisdom embedded throughout my physical environment.

How might I employ the techniques of the Wisdom scientist and discern innate Wisdom in Nature?

If I look out to sea and discern the horizon, or view the expanses of a mountain range, I might discern that the laws that sustain order on this planet are governed by Innate Wisdom, that the forces that transformed the face of Earth over millions of years are programmed by the Innate Wisdom that has determined the structure of the physical environment I can see before me. Every step I take is governed by the law of gravity that, in turn, is governed by Innate Wisdom.

If I am Wisdom-conscious, I am aware that, according to the Wisdom school, an Innate Wisdom governs not only animate beings around me, but also all inanimate realms.

Our Wisdom consciousness may even be aroused when we face storms clouds.

In Chapter Three, we learned that Wisdom is incarnate in all forms of life, all stages of evolution. The dilemma we face in our Western world is that we humans have treated all life-forms—other than human beings—as objects of investigation rather than fellow Earth beings, as inferior beings rather than intelligent beings possessing Incarnate Wisdom.

If I now walk through my garden, a rainforest or a wild wilderness, I am surrounded by numerous forms of life: everything from echidnas to amoeba, from giant eucalypts to wallabies. Beneath my feet are life-forms in the soil and the sand. Above my head there are life-forms in the atmosphere and beyond. If I am Wisdom-aware, I am conscious of Wisdom incarnate—or if you will, wired—within each of these life-forms, even the smallest ant.

The questions posed by the voice from the whirlwind are designed to activate my discernment so that I become conscious of the presence of Wisdom throughout the cosmos.

The Wonder Called Wisdom

The experience of Wisdom consciousness may be tantamount to spiritual awareness for some of the 'would-be-wise' observing nature or exploring the cosmos. I suggest, however, that the response of Job to his Wisdom-consciousness experience may offer another dimension of spiritual awareness.

Job's ultimate challenge was to comprehend how all the realms where Wisdom was a driving force contributed to the 'design' of the cosmos. The Wisdom consciousness that Job acquires is indeed a form of 'cosmic consciousness'. But is his new awareness also a 'spiritual experience'?

Job's response to his tour of the cosmos is perhaps surprising (Job 42:1–6). He recognises that the voice from the whirlwind is challenging him to understand the *'etsa*: the primordial design, the Wisdom blueprint for the cosmos. Job admits that he had not used his 'discernment'— his Incarnate Wisdom—to interpret the mysteries of the cosmos, or understand what is happening in his physical world.

Previously, he had focused on the question: Where can justice be found? Now he is faced with the question: Where can Wisdom be found? He declares:

> I heard of you with my ears,
> but now my eyes 'see' you (Job 42:5).

What does Job mean when he claims 'my eyes see you'? Surely such a cry is an admission that he has now had a spiritual experience of some kind. What kind of experience? The context is the Wisdom school; the meaning of this pivotal cry is relevant to our understanding of his response.

In the past, my response—before listening closely to the Wisdom narrator—was that Job was claiming to 'see' God, a celestial being with whom he became familiar through his tour of the cosmos.

A close reading of Job's journey, however, reveals that he is never challenged to 'see' God as a celestial being present throughout the cosmos. The focus of the questions is on the origins, operations and mysteries of the cosmos. The common factor in the exploration of these realms of the cosmos is the role of Primordial, Innate and Incarnate Wisdom.

A significant feature of Job's response is his use of the term *ra'a* (see/observe). As I noted in the Introduction, this verb is a technical term in the Wisdom school. A key step for the wise scientist of old was to 'see' or 'observe' a particular phenomenon closely to 'discern' its essential nature.

Job, the newly initiated wise scientist, now claims 'my eyes see/observe you'. But who, what, where is this 'you'? Or, in the language of the Wisdom school: 'What has Job 'observed' by close examination?

The initial assertion of the voice from the whirlwind is that someone—namely Job—has been obscuring primordial Wisdom, the 'design' of the cosmos (Job 38:2). Following this pronouncement, the divine mentor leads Job across the cosmos—from primordial realms to the world of wild animals. Job is challenged to discern the presence of Wisdom encoded in all the laws and realms of the universe.

The divine mentor does not challenge Job specifically to see or discern God in these domains. Job, nevertheless, claims: 'my eyes have seen you'.

Job's education in the world of cosmic Wisdom is comprehensive. Job has clearly 'seen' and 'discerned' Wisdom as a force in all realms of nature at the end of his master class. Job has acquired a Wisdom consciousness: an awareness that Wisdom is a wondrous spiritual presence that can be 'seen' and discerned by a Wisdom-conscious human.

In short, I would now contend that the 'you' Job observes is the presence and power permeating the cosmos: Primordial, Innate and Incarnate Wisdom. Job 'sees' Wisdom with more than intellectual insight; Job discerns that Wisdom is the cosmic spiritual presence that 'fills' the cosmos.

Afterthought

I have long heard
'the Triune God is omnipresent in the world'
but now I discover
'that the Wisdom Trinity is omnipresent in creation'!

Chapter Five
Wisdom Spirituality

Wisdom spirituality involves alerting our Wisdom
consciousness to deep dimensions of the Wisdom Trinity that
can be identified as spiritual.

Cosmic Mysteries

Responding to the mysteries of the cosmos that Job is
challenged to 'discern' in the opening questions posed by
our Wisdom mentor, may involve more than acknowledg-
ing the limits of our Wisdom consciousness in the past
(Job 42:3). Our response, like that of Job, may involve a
deep spiritual dimension, as Job recognises (Job 42:4–6).

The cosmos is filled with mysteries reflecting the presence and operating power of primordial Wisdom. At this
point, having gained as appreciation of the experience
of Job, we can recognise the spiritual dimension of these
mysteries. Whether the mystery relates to the black holes
in space, the origin of planet Earth, the explosion of the
Big Bang, Wisdom is the spiritual presence that precedes
and activates the mystery. Wisdom is the mother of mysteries, the spiritual presence that confronts us when we
seek to discern the meaning and force of a mystery.

The Spiritual is the silent Wisdom impulse of Wisdom present in all the phenomena of the cosmos.

If we now listen again to our Wisdom mentor, can we hear the call to alert our Wisdom consciousness and discern the spiritual in the space that surround us;

Scan the Skies

Can you stand under the sky late at night,
gaze deep into space and back into time
observing distant stars, local planets and the blanks beyond?

Before you is the mystery of the entire cosmos:
a vast universe of matter and anti-matter,
a world of lights coming from explosions,
many of which occurred billions of years ago.

Can you, via a telescope,
observe the collage of distant images
forming patterns and designs that span time and space,
that take you back to the primordial?

Before you is Wisdom: the blueprint of creation,
the design of the cosmos,
the ultimate spiritual mystery,
that takes you back to the very beginning of creation
before any Big Bang or Soft Whisper.

You are connected to that beginning:
a tiny piece of matter
surviving in an ancient cosmic design
called Wisdom.

Can you now take a spiritual leap of faith,
reach back to read the primal blueprint,
to discern the mystery of cosmic Wisdom
before your very eyes?

> Can you now connect
> with the spiritual mystery of the cosmos,
> aware that your Wisdom consciousness
> enables you to discern primordial Wisdom,
> the spiritual blueprint of creation?

Natural Wonders

The challenge we face here is to discern levels of response to the wonders of Wisdom in nature that are personally deep and meaningful—levels that reflect spiritual experience rather than traditional knowledge.

One way of responding to an experience of Innate Wisdom as a mystery in nature is a sense of awe—whether as quiet amazement or sheer wonder. To be in the presence of such a pervading mystery may cause us to be mesmerised in amazement.

The challenge of such a wonder may move us to delve even deeper into a phenomenon filled with mystery and seek for meaning or ultimate causes.

A profound Wisdom-related experience that the scribes of the Wisdom school discerned was also sometimes described in terms of wonder. The wise in Proverbs declare:

> Three things are a great wonder for me,
> four I do not understand:
> the way of the eagle in the sky,
> the way of a snake on a rock,
> the way of a ship on the sea,
> and the way of a man with a girl (Proverbs 30:18–19).

Sages may have found many things just too amazing to contemplate (Proverbs 30:18–28). Job may have felt so small before the wonders of the cosmos that he clapped his hand on his mouth and admitted there were mysteries beyond his comprehension (Job 40:4; 42:3). The author of Ecclesiastes may have found Wisdom to be nothing short of 'sheer mystery', or the ultimate 'enigma' (*hebel*) (Eccles. 1:12–18).

Wonder is recognised as a spiritual response to the experience of Wisdom in nature.

Scientists may be struck with wonder as they contemplate the origins of the universe. The very design of the cosmos evokes sheer amazement amongst nuclear physicists. They are likewise astounded by the very existence of atoms when it might be expected that all matter and corresponding antimatter would cancel each other out and leave but a glow of cosmic radiation (Deane-Drummond, 2006, 22).

If we now listen again to our Wisdom mentor, can we hear the call to alert our Wisdom consciousness and discern the spiritual in the natural wonders that surround us, wonders like a threatening black thunderstorm.

Face the Storm Clouds

Today I am asking you to stand
on the balcony of your house looking out to sea.
In the distance, over the ocean,
a massive black wall of clouds is slowly rolling
over the waters to overwhelm you.

As you watch,
you are looking through a window of wonder.
An eerie
stillness and silence surrounds you.
As you watch, a frightening black wall of violent clouds
is rolling closer and closer,
about to explode in your face.

Remember the question posed
by the Wisdom scientist:

Where can Wisdom be found?
The answer is staring you in the face.
Where can Wisdom be found?
In the great weight of water
suspended in the cloud about to burst upon you!
In the force of the wild wind in the storm
whose impact we are about to feel!
In the laws of nature that guide the rain
to fall on the sea and on the soil before us!
In the way of the lightning and thunder
crashing onto the scene before us!

What a wonder!
What a spiritual surprise!

The Wisdom scientist found Wisdom
in the 'way' of the thunderstorm:
the inner code that guides all dimensions
of our seasons and our weather.

And today you too can discern Wisdom
encoded in the thunderstorm
in the same way,
if you are Wisdom conscious
and spiritually aware
of the wonders of Wisdom in nature.

Spiritual Compass

Profound as these experiences may be, we may ask whether they could lead to a spiritual awareness or a spiritual experience. *A priori*, we need to recognise that 'spiritual awareness'— or 'spiritual experience' in the Wisdom tradition—may differ from that in the prophetic world or in the Pentecostal tradition. Prophets may have a religious experience when they claim to be confronted by the voice of God. People in Pentecostal communities may claim to experience forms of ecstasy or transportation into another world.

The experience of sheer wonder or Wisdom consciousness, however, is a spiritual experience of a different nature. The goal: to stir our Wisdom consciousness so that our Wisdom compass becomes aware of the spiritual dimension of reality in the Wisdom in, with and under our world. As we noted above, Job's Wisdom consciousness is aroused by the persistent questions of the Wisdom mentor until he confesses that he has experienced 'Wisdom' as a spiritual presence.

If we now listen again to our Wisdom mentor, can we hear the call to alert our Wisdom consciousness and discern the spiritual in the living creatures of the cosmos, everything from ants to antelopes, hippopotamuses to humans.

Observe the Ants

Walk through the woods until you find
an ants' nest alive with ants.

Observe the ants
and try to discern the 'way' of the ant:
the Wisdom compass incarnate in the ant.

If you follow the advice of the Wisdom mentor,
whose observations are recorded in Proverbs,
you may discern the amazing capacity of ants
to operate without any leader:
they know intuitively how to gather
during the summer the food needed for winter.

And if we observe a little longer
we are faced with many other incarnate capacities
that are dimensions of the Wisdom of ants:
the spiritual within living creatures.

Watch them follow a common path
from food sources in the garden and back to the nest.
Watch them greet each other
as they meet on the their pathways,
communicating their presence and purpose.

Observe
the intensification of their speed and activity
when a rainstorm in impending
or a danger is near.

By discerning the 'way' of the ant
you discern a dimension of Wisdom:
an incarnate life-force that is typical and true
of all living creatures
and has existed since they first evolved,
a silent impulse called
the spiritual.

Connect with the Navel

Please stand with me at sunset
facing a massive rock, a mile high
and twenty miles around.

The rock is Uluru,
a golden boulder rising from the red centre of Australia—
a sacred site of local Aboriginal peoples
and all who discern Wisdom
in nature.

As we watch, the rock explodes with wonder,
changing colour from instant to instant—
from celestial gold to earthy orange,
from vivid bronze to blazing red—
all the colours of a desert rainbow!

We sense what many have sensed
in other lands before us:

that concentration point of the spiritual—
the navel of Earth
where the spiritual is incarnate in the soil,
where the intrinsic worth of Earth
is revealed in wonder,
in a rock,
and in our consciousness.

The navel of Earth
connects us with the birth of Earth,
the beginnings of the cosmos,
the very blueprint of the universe,
with the Wisdom innate in this place—
the natural force that designed the universe
in which Earth is born
and shows us the navel
of her existence as a sacred site,
a spiritual wonder
of the cosmos.

A Wisdom Discernment Song

(Melody: *Morning Has Broken*. Words: Norman Habel, 7 September 2018)

As a way of celebrating the spiritual dimensions of Wisdom, we may sing this song and hear the voice of our Wisdom Mentor reminding is that Wisdom is waiting for us to discern her spiritual presence pulsing throughout creation, reminding us:

Wisdom is waiting deep in creation,
Wisdom innate in all that we see,
Wisdom is calling throughout the cosmos:
'Time to revive an old mystery'.

Time to examine Wisdom's dimensions:
first we discern her cosmic design,
then the strong impulse in all that's living,
and the deep wonder stirring our mind.

Wisdom was present from the beginning,
filling the world with grand cosmic laws;
she is the blueprint mapped in creation,
she is the primal deep cosmic cause.

She is the drive in all that's evolving,
creating codes in all that exists;
she is the lifeline found in creation,
pulsing through forests, oceans and mists.

Wisdom is more than knowledge or learning;
she is the soul, the compass, the drive,
keeping us true to our inner nature;
she is the reason we are alive.

Wisdom is more than quotes from the Bible;
she is the soul, the mystery so deep;
she is the spirit, throughout the cosmos;
she is the song that makes our hearts leap.

Chapter Six
Wisdom Experiences

Experiences of Wisdom consciousness and Wisdom
spirituality can be captured in poetry based on Wisdom
discernment.

Responding to the mysteries of the cosmos I became
aware of myself as an Earth being endowed with an innate
capacity to 'discern' Wisdom in my world, in my environment and in my inner self. A selection of the poems that
reflect my experiences follow as guidelines for would-
be Wisdom scientists to go beyond contemplation to
'observe', 'discern' and 'discover' Wisdom spirituality.

The Cosmic Me

When the space age
burst in upon my consciousness
and shattered my image of the world,
I became small: so small,
like a pinprick on a planet,
a human footnote
in the never ending story of the universe.
Then, one morning,
after watching the sunrise,

I awakened to the dawn of the cosmos
breaking through my brain.
I am now conscious
of discerning my being
as a climax of the cosmos evolving
into the mystery called me
endowed with Wisdom
and wonder.

Cosmic Blueprint

God's special relationship with Wisdom
is reflected in Proverbs 8.
The voice of Wisdom declares:
YHWH acquired me first,
his way before his works.

This declaration challenged me for years:
Wisdom preceding creation,
Mystery 'acquiring' Wisdom—
the necessary design
for creation.

Wisdom claiming to be
the blueprint for creation:
the innate force
guaranteeing the design,
character,
function
of all creation—
everything
from the Big Bang
to the tiny touch
facilitating
the origins of life.

Wow!
Wisdom is tantamount
to the innate Spirituality

that determines
the character:
the 'way'
of the entire cosmos.

Discerning the Primordial

Setting the scene:
The date: 8 March 1986.
The place: a mountain in Tamil Nadu, South India.
The event: Halley's comet visible on Earth—next opportunity:
28 July 2061.
The participants: scientists, scribes, students—and me.

We are drawn together to observe Halley's comet,
completing its long, spectacular perihelion circuit;
a return to planet Earth's skies—
a seventy-six-year cosmic scenic journey,
repeated *ad infinitum.*

We look up: the comet moves across the sky,
leaving its long trail of icy gases;
a genuine piece of stardust before our eyes,
bright light, high above us,
sharing a once-in-my-lifetime vision of timeless space travel!

The comet appears before us—a classroom model
coming alive before our eyes:
a microcosm of the universe;
an image of the cosmos in miniature;
matter and energy and mystery in endless motion
from the beginning of time
to the moment the comet appears before us,
in human time,
and leaves us, gasping at Primordial mystery,
on display, a glorious vision of habitual transit—
an endless journeying, for its own purpose.

The comet appears,
parading its glory:
a microcosm of Primordial Wisdom—
the design of the universe,
reflected in the image of the comet spinning across the sky,
a glory cloud, for our eyes to discern.
Amazed, we discern an image of Wisdom:
the blueprint of the cosmos—
displayed for our pleasure and delight—
just because . . .

A blueprint dazzling and dynamic;
a blueprint shimmering with primal intelligence;
a blueprint wired for motion and mystery—
a blueprint that evokes sheer wonder
and awakens a vivid cosmic consciousness.

Connecting with a Cradle

As I walk among of the mountains
of the Flinders Ranges in South Australia,
I see a ridge that runs along one of the ranges.
I discover that ridge is, in fact,
a mass of stromatolites—
very early forms of life that evolved under the sea
that once covered these ranges.

When I hold one of these fossilised life-forms
in the palm of my hand,
I realise I am holding the beginnings of life:
babies 600 million years old.
I am amazed—
not only by the mystery of such early life-forms,
but also by a sense of sheer wonder of how Wisdom
determined the innate nature of these creatures,
emerging in the depths of the oceans,
and preserving them for me to hold today.

I could have interpreted that moment in many ways,
but I discern that I am connected
with the very origins of life
on our Mother, Earth.
It is a sacred moment to be treasured,
an experience that is spiritual.

These babies
are among our earliest relatives on Earth,
relatives whose identity is determined
by Wisdom
innate in the Flinders Ranges.

Amazing!

Innate Wisdom

With my focus on acquired wisdom
I read the Wisdom books,
Proverbs or Job;
acquired wisdom
is learned wisdom from my elders
from observing human behaviour.

The ancient world wise ones, however,
observed and explored Wisdom
in every realm
of nature;
creation's animate and inanimate components—
everyone has an innate 'way'
and a designated 'place' in the cosmos.

The writer of Proverbs tells me to
'observe'
the 'way' of the ant
and get Wisdom!
Every creature
—ant, bee, echidna, wombat—
has a 'way';

an innate capacity to be
true to its nature, its essential being.

What then is my 'way'
my innate nature
as an Earth being,
a human being,
a spiritual being?

That was once my question.
My answer now:
'observe;
discern;
activate you 'way',
your Incarnate Wisdom.

Turtle Wisdom

Born in the sand
on the Queensland coast of Australia,
a baby sea turtle
scrambles across the beach
impelled by an impulse
to swim,
swim out to sea
into the deep
alone,
no mother to mentor,
no parent to protect,
swim sixteen years
alone,
twenty thousand miles
alone,
come back home
to hover ten years more,
to mate,
to lay her eggs hoping that
one day

one baby may reach that shore
wired with Incarnate Wisdom
no human baby
born alone
on this beach
could ever know.

DNA

What do we say
to the mystery of DNA—
that intelligent cue in each pool of genes.
From early evolution
DNA means:
like produces like,
sweet produces sweet,
sour produces sour.

What do we say
about the mystery of DNA
when we discover a dubious twist:
the DNA of an elephant
is almost the same
as the DNA of a platypus.

Early explorers sent
the first platypus samples to Britain
to be classified.
The scientists denied
their very existence.

Is it the platypus that tricks us all:
swimming like a fish,
with a beak like a duck,
a baby in its pouch,
DNA like an elephant?

Or is it the Wisdom
innate in the sapient DNA

reminding us all to observe
more than the weird,
to grasp the mystery of DNA,
otherwise known as Wisdom?

Godwit Wisdom

Recently, seated on a grassy area
near a shoreline of a bay
in Auckland, New Zealand.
Waiting and watching
I observed
hundreds of bar-tailed godwits gathering,
racing around in a feeding frenzy
communicating with extreme agitation.

Suddenly,
heeding a signal deep within,
they began to circle
forming a spiral of spinning life.
Slowly the spiral swirled out to sea,
the godwits setting out across the ocean,
flying across vast waters,
through storms over the equator,
on their way to a chosen location in Siberia
where they feed, breed,
nurture their young
before they return to Auckland.

At that moment I could sense their Wisdom,
the Wisdom of flight and the Wisdom of memory,
encoded in their spirits.
I discerned an amazing intelligence
of fellow Land beings
guiding themselves non-stop
to a place across the ocean
more than ten thousand kilometres away!

I had discerned Wisdom in nature,
that incarnate force driving their evolution
over millions of years.

Cosmic Journey

When I journey through the cosmos
with Job and my Wisdom Mentor.
I am astounded
at how my understanding of ecology
and ancient Wisdom
are deeply interrelated.

As I follow Job and my Wisdom mentor
back to the origins of Planet Earth,
the depths of the underworld
and the designated 'places' of light and darkness,
I am amazed as I discern
in response to the Mentor's question,
how the laws of space—
the Wisdom forces in the skies—
establish order on Planet Earth.

Planet Earth is connected
astrologically and ecologically.
Laws of space
establish Earth's unique way.
Earth: a living eco-system
activated by Wisdom.

And I, as an Earth being,
am interconnected with space,
with the Wisdom laws of the universe.

I am a land being,
a human on planet Earth
with cosmic eco-consciousness,
Wisdom consciousness
and land consciousness.

Moment of Truth: Job 42:1–6

After his long journey through the cosmos
and the world of the wild,
Job declares
he will not pursue his case against God;
he will leave behind his dust and ashes,
his devastating trauma location.

Why?
Because, he says, 'my eyes have seen God'.

Amazing!
In viewing all the domains of the cosmos—
specifically
discerning innate Wisdom forces
governing these realms—
Job claims to 'see' God.

Realising 'seeing'
is a technical Wisdom school term
for 'observing' a phenomenon of nature,
we recognise Job's comment is
not poetic idiom,
not pious metaphor.

Job discovers God is not a being
harassing him from heaven.
Job observes Innate Wisdom forces
operating in each realm of the universe;
for Job God is the Wisdom
present in the cosmos.

Chapter Seven
Wisdom Confession

Reflecting anew on
the challenges of my Wisdom mentor
from the ancient Wisdom school
and
the profound questions of the Wisdom narrator
in the book of Job,
I believe I am bold enough to make the following
confession
even if it sounds like heresy.

I now believe that Wisdom
is primary
and that all portrayals of God
by the religions of the world
are secondary.

I am now conscious of Wisdom
as a positive spiritual impulse
that is omnipresent
and has been active
since the beginning of time.

I believe that Wisdom
is the primal 'way', the cosmic blueprint,
the silent spiritual impulse,

the features of whose design of the cosmos
are discernible in the mysteries and wonders
of the universe
captured by artists, thinkers and scientists.
I believe that Wisdom
is also a primal system of codes
throughout the natural world
whose innate laws govern
the 'ways' of nature,
the mystery called ecology.

I believe that Wisdom
in the spiritual life force
incarnate in all living things,
a life force
discernible even by geologists
gardeners, psychologists
and poets.

I believe that Wisdom
is a silent impulse incarnate in human beings
that stirs human consciousness
to both reach out to connect with cosmic Wisdom
and Wisdom in the natural order,
and also to enable each person
to be true to his or her innate 'way'
as a human being.

I believe Wisdom is the spiritual core
of the cosmos,
our planet,
and my inner being,
a spiritual core that activates my self
to be true to
the Wisdom presence that surrounds me
and guides me
to be open-minded and open-hearted,
and to live fairly, justly and wisely
in tune with cosmic Wisdom, the 'ways' of nature
and my Incarnate Wisdom consciousness.

Wisdom is also another name
for the natural 'laws'
on how to be custodians
of creation,
that the First Nations of Australia
'discern'
when they read the landscape
and 'see'
the spiritual.

Yes,
Wisdom is deeper than doctrine
more relevant than traditional religion,
and
more spiritual than mild meditation
or the pious prayers
addressed to a celestial deity
or forgotten mystery.

One final confession.
When I am faced with a crisis,
an important decision,
a broken relationship
or deep question
I do not pray to be saved
by a being on high,
scream bloody murder
as I once did like Job
or
muse over a dangerous doctrine,

Now
I activate my Incarnate Wisdom,
my spiritual core,
the true inner me
to be free
to observe the truth of the situation,
to discern how to act faithfully
and empathetically

in tune with
the Incarnate Wisdom
that stirs my consciousness
and
keeps me alive.
and Wisdom-conscious.

Wisdom Blessing

May the Wisdom
that permeates and activates
the cosmos
activate your consciousness
and make you aware
that you are
a piece of Wisdom stardust.

May the Wisdom
that governs and guides
the laws and forces of nature
stir your awareness
and make you conscious
that you are ecologically connected
with every atom
on the earth

May the Wisdom
incarnate in your very being
come alive deep within you
and make you Wisdom conscious,
a living being
animated
and activated
by a spiritual mystery
called Wisdom.

Wisdom Epilogue

*retrieved from the Prologue
of the Gospel of St John.*

In the beginning was Wisdom
and the Wisdom was with God,
and Wisdom was the blueprint
God employed in the design
and creation of the cosmos.

And God ensured that innate Wisdom
functioned effectively
in the laws and forces of Nature.

In the creation process
God confirmed that Wisdom was incarnate
in all living creatures
including human beings.
And we can discern that Wisdom
in the way
of Jesus of Nazareth.

Norman Habel

Bibliography

Deane-Drummond, Celia. *Wisdom and Wonder. Conversations in Science, Spirituality and Theology* (Philadelphia: Templeton Foundation Press, 2006).

Flannery, Tim, *Here on Earth. An Argument for Hope* (Melbourne: Text Publishing, 2010).

Habel, Norman, *Yahweh Versus Baal. A Conflict of Religious Cultures* (New York: Bookman Associates, 1964).

_____ 'The Symbolism of Wisdom in Proverbs 1-9', in *Interpretation*, 26 (1972), 131–57.

_____ *The Book of Job. A Commentary* (Philadelphia: Westminster Press, 1985).

_____ 'In Defence of God the Sage' in *The Voice from the Whirlwind*, edited by Leo Perdue & W Clark Gilpin (New York: Abingdon, 1992), 21–38.

_____ 'Is the wild Ox Willing To Serve You? Challenging the Mandate to Dominate' in *The Earth Story in Wisdom Traditions*, The Earth Bible, Volume 3, edited by Norman Habel & Shirley Wurst (Sheffield: Sheffield Academic Press, 2001), 179–89.

_____ 'The Implications of God Discovering Wisdom in Earth' in *Job 28: Cognition in Context*, edited by Ellen van Wolde (Leiden: Brill, 2003), 281–98.

63

_____ *An Inconvenient Text. Is a Green Reading of the Bible Possible?* (Adelaide: ATF Press, 2009).

_____ *The Birth, the Curse and the Greening of Earth*: *An Ecological Reading of Genesis 1–11* (Sheffield: Sheffield Phoenix Press, 2011).

_____ *Rainbow of Mysteries. Meeting the Sacred in Nature* (Kelowna: Copperhouse, 2012).

_____ 'The Way of Things! Earth-Wisdom and Climate Change' in *Climate Change Cultural Change. Religious Responses and Responsibilities,* edited by Anne Elvey & David Gormley-O'Brien (Melbourne: Mosaic Press, 2013), 1–10.

_____ *Finding Wisdom in Nature. An Ecological Reading of the Book of Job* (Sheffield: Sheffield Phoenix Press, 2014).

_____ *Discerning Wisdom in God's Creation* (Northcote: Morning Star, 2015).

_____ *Acknowledgement of the Land and Faith of Aboriginal Custodians after Following the Abraham Trail* (Northcote: Morning Star, 2018).

Kalugila, Leonidas, *The Wise King. Studies in Royal Wisdom as Divine Revelation in the Old Testament and Its Environment* (Gleerup: AMS Press, 1980).

Lenzi, Alan, 'Proverbs 8:22–31: Three Perspectives on Its Composition', in *JBL* 125 (2006), 687–714.

McKane, William, *Proverbs*, The Old Testament Library (Philadelphia: Westminster, 1970).

Whybray, RN, *Wisdom in Proverbs* (London: SCM Press, 1965).

CPSIA information can be obtained
at www.ICGtesting.com
Printed in the USA
LVHW030126210421
685055LV00001B/15